Love's Ways

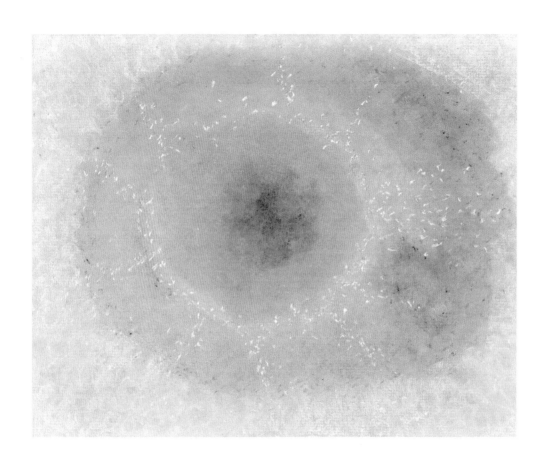

Love's Ways

A Meditation on Love

Mark Gabriele

Pastels by Kazzrie Jaxen

MIRAMBEL

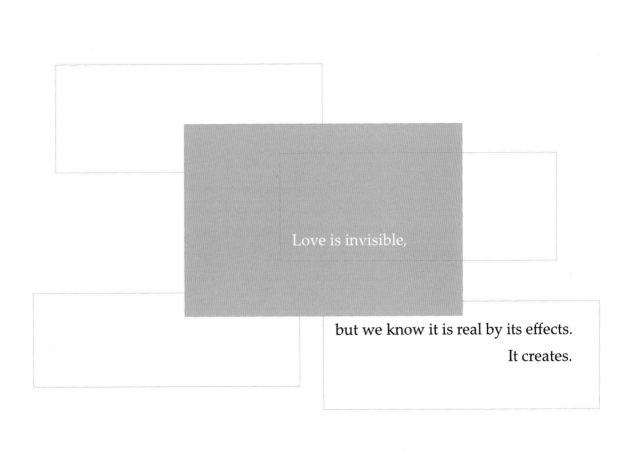

Love is invisible,

but we know it is real by its effects.
It creates.

What it creates is more love

for where love is offered,

love is returned.

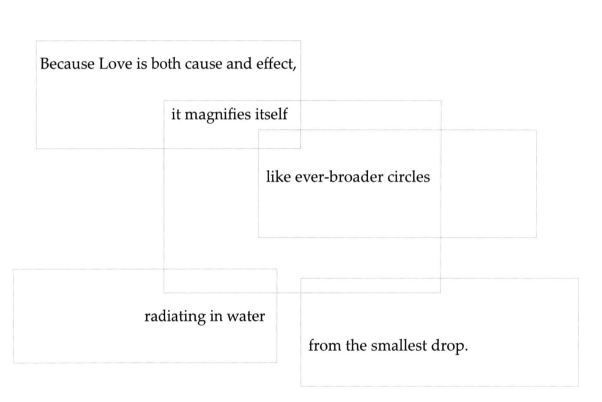

Because Love is both cause and effect,

it magnifies itself

like ever-broader circles

radiating in water

from the smallest drop.

Love's eyes are different than ours.

They do not discern or discriminate as ours do. Love sees with the heart and recognizes only its own creations as real.

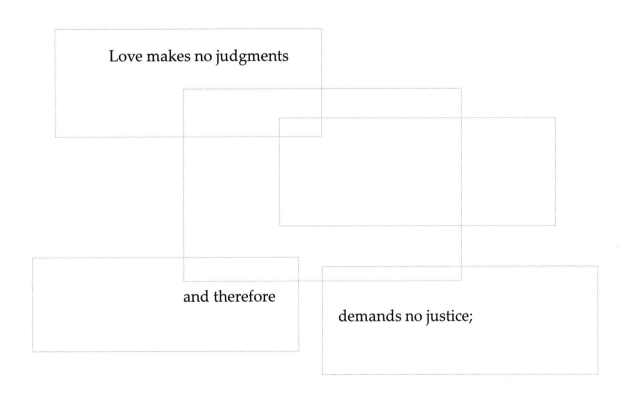

Love makes no judgments

and therefore

demands no justice;

Where there are boundaries

it seeks to bridge them,

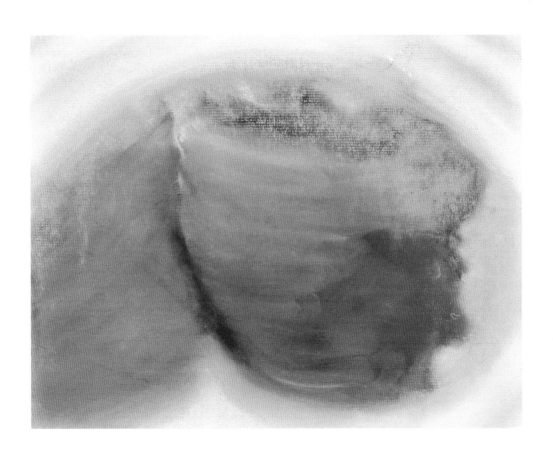

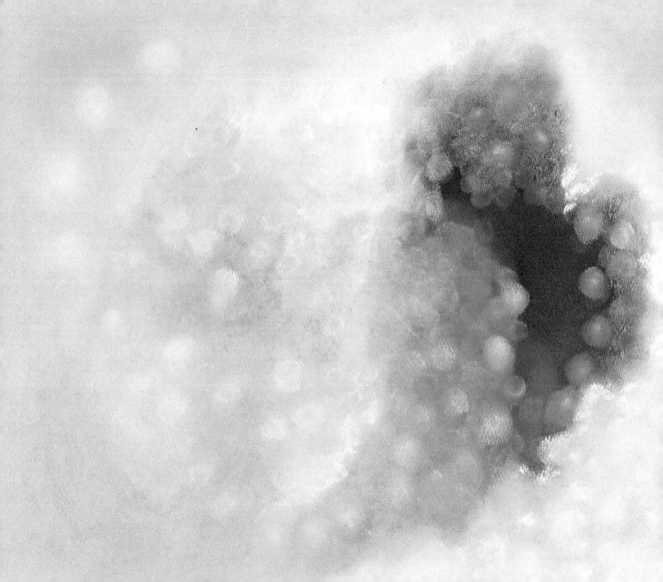

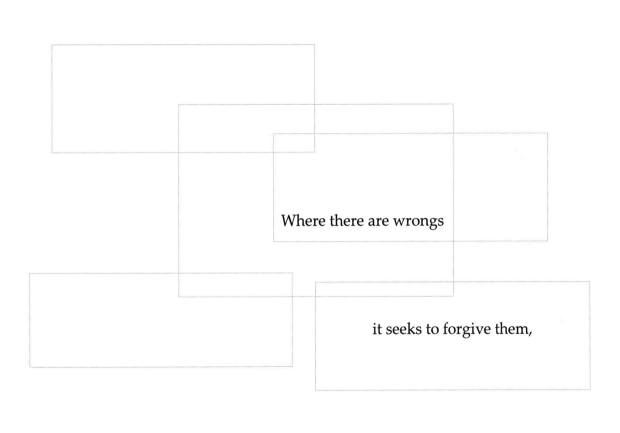

Where there are wrongs

it seeks to forgive them,

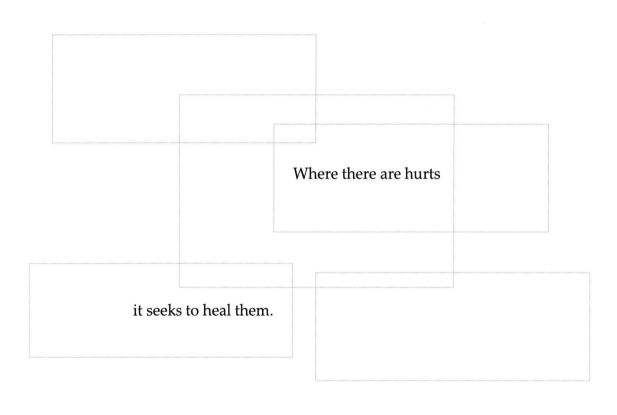

Where there are hurts

it seeks to heal them.

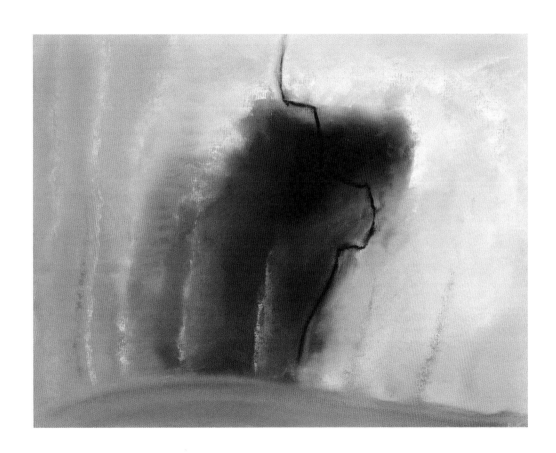

Love does not know time as we do—

something that extinguishes itself
passing from an uncertain future
into an irreversible past.

For Love, time

like everything else,

has but one purpose—

to increase love.

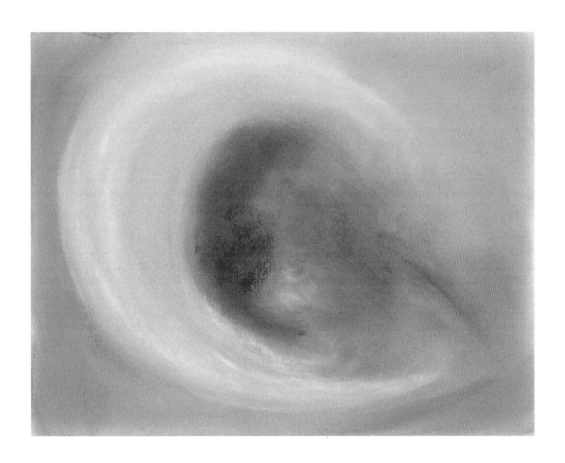

Therefore Love knows only one time,

the time when there is complete
freedom for creation,
the present moment.

Fleeting for us,

it is eternal for Love.

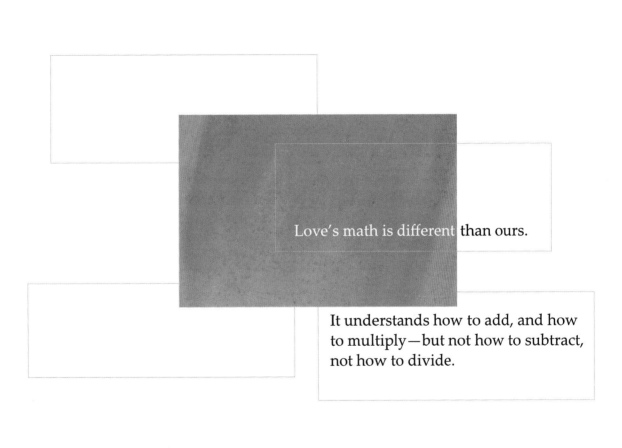

Love's math is different than ours.

It understands how to add, and how to multiply—but not how to subtract, not how to divide.

When it adds, it always makes one.

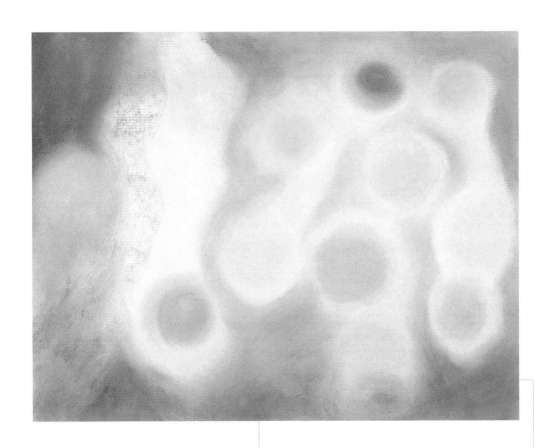

What it adds, it multiplies.

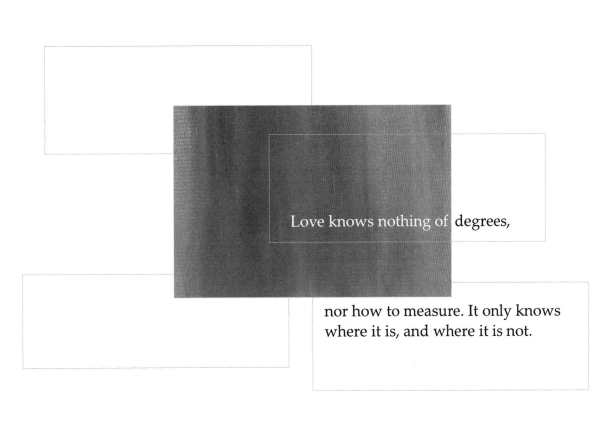

Love knows nothing of degrees, nor how to measure. It only knows where it is, and where it is not.

Where it is not, it longs to be created

and where it has been lost,

it longs to be restored.

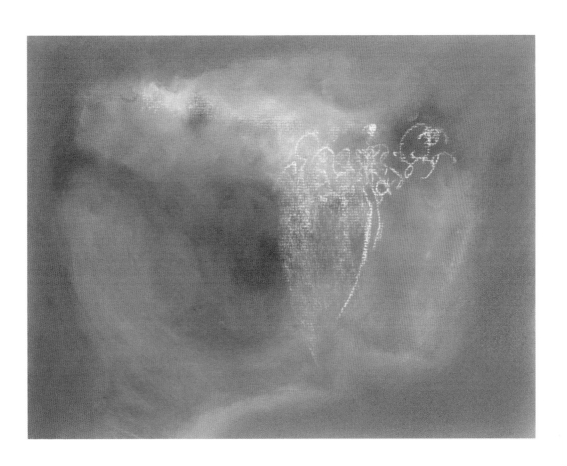

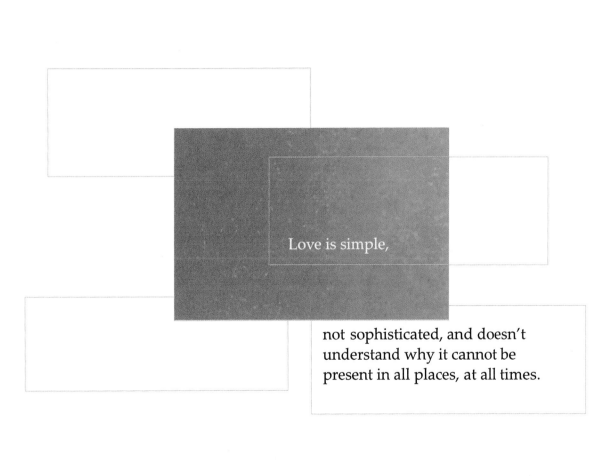

Love is simple,

not sophisticated, and doesn't understand why it cannot be present in all places, at all times.

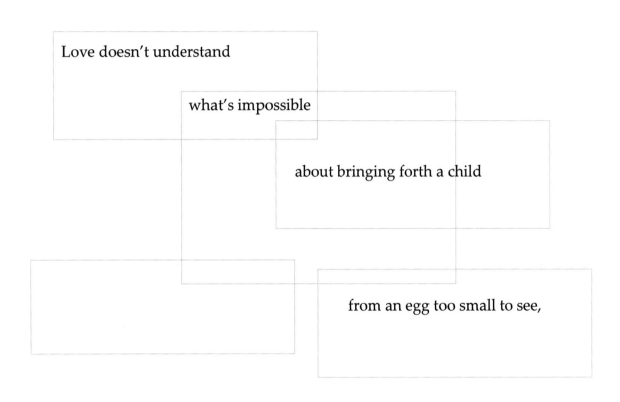

Love doesn't understand

what's impossible

about bringing forth a child

from an egg too small to see,

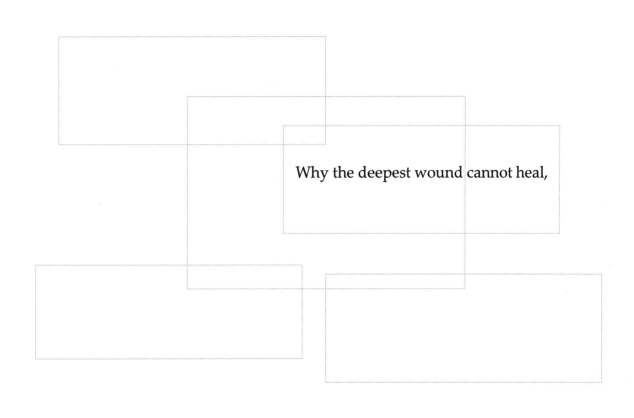

Why the deepest wound cannot heal,

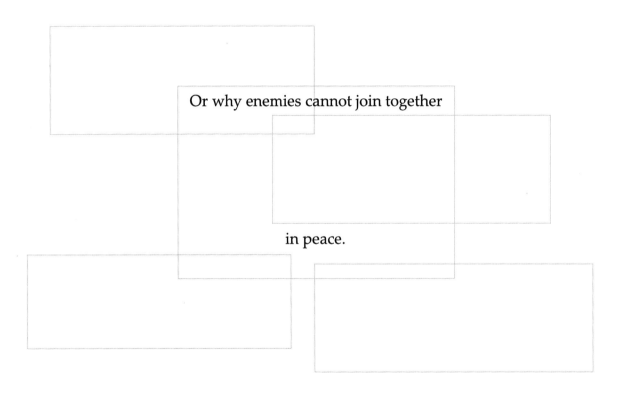

Or why enemies cannot join together

in peace.

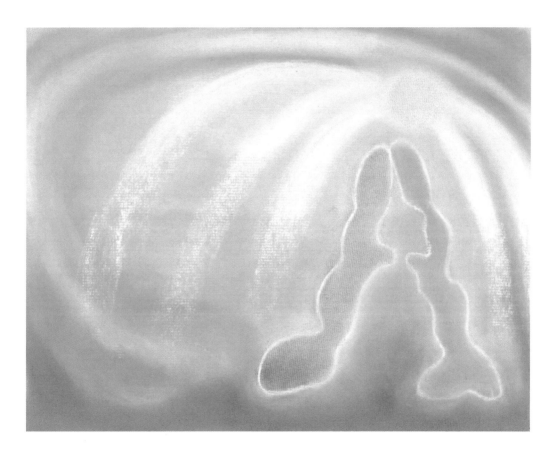

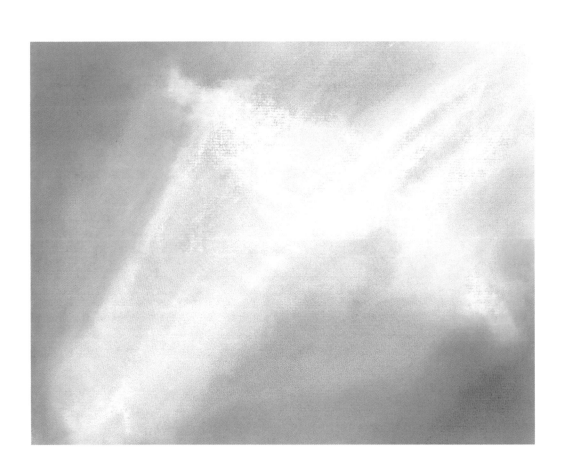

These things defy our sense
of the world, so for us
are miraculous.

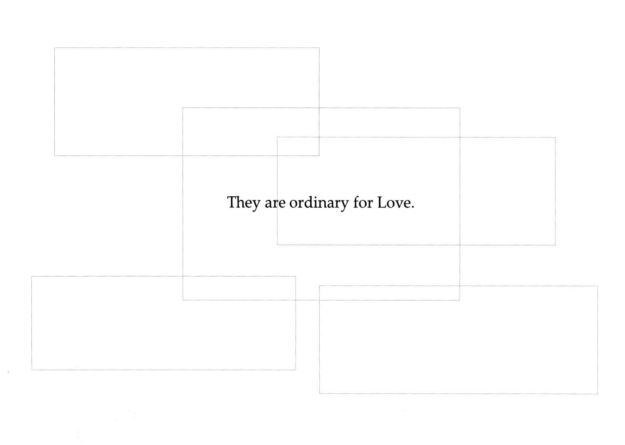

They are ordinary for Love.

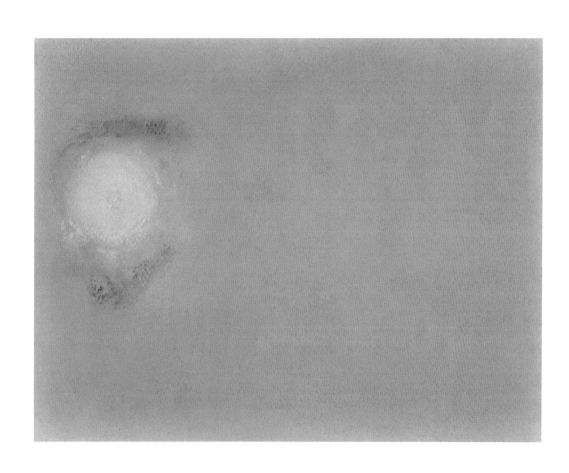

Love fulfills who we are,

and what we really want.

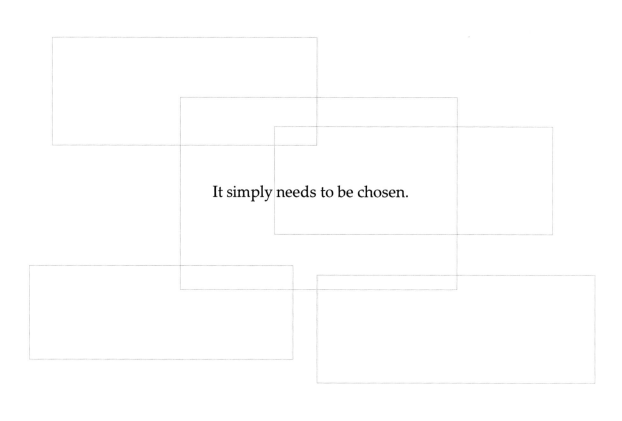

It simply needs to be chosen.

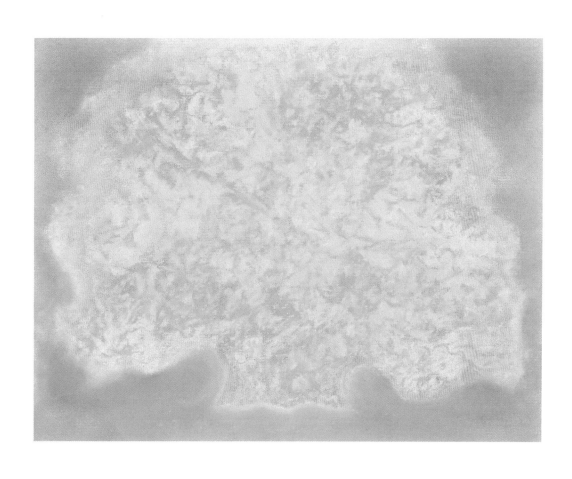

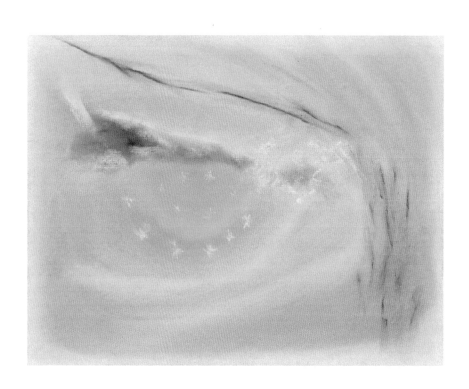

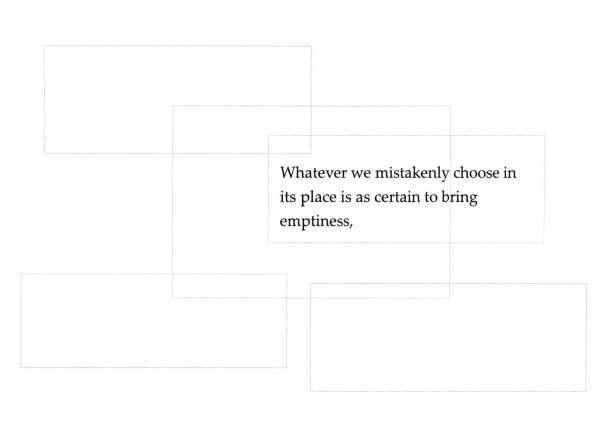

Whatever we mistakenly choose in its place is as certain to bring emptiness,

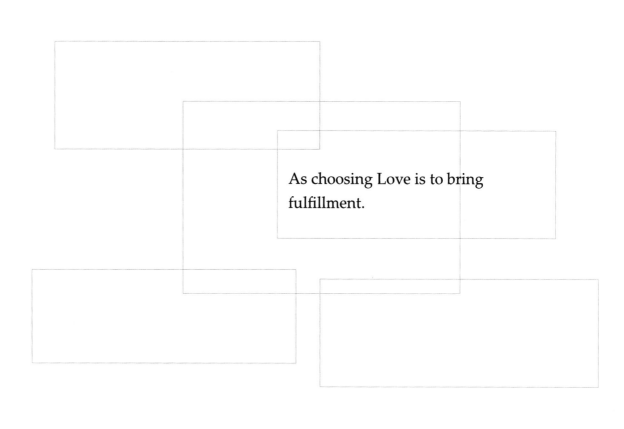

As choosing Love is to bring fulfillment.

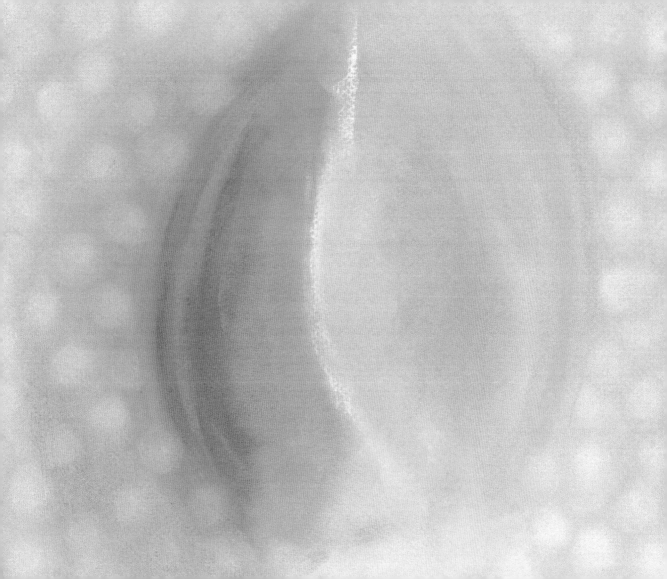

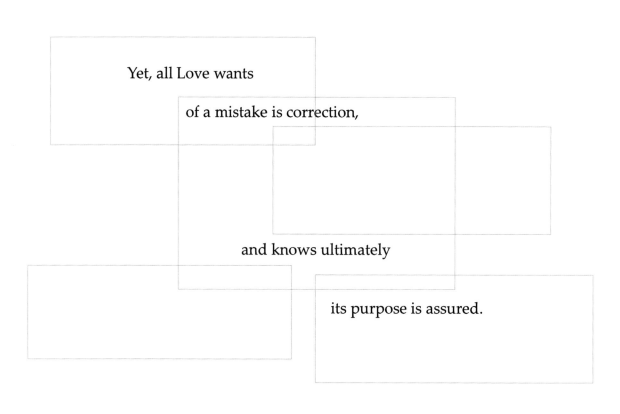

Yet, all Love wants

of a mistake is correction,

and knows ultimately

its purpose is assured.

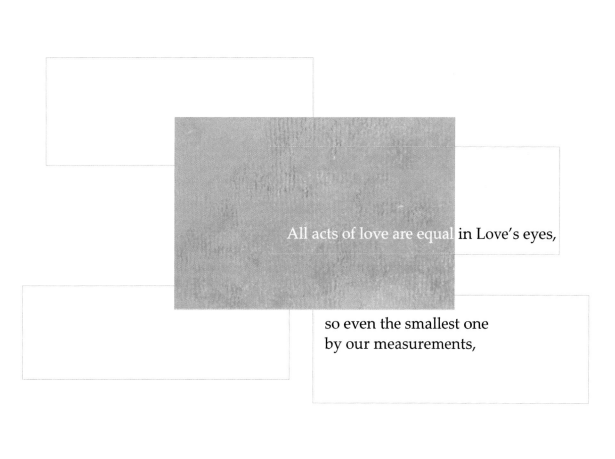

All acts of love are equal in Love's eyes,

so even the smallest one
by our measurements,

is enough

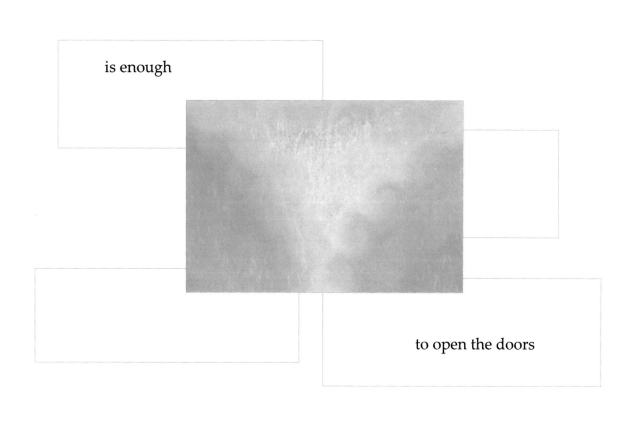

to open the doors

to All of Heaven.

Love's Ways
A Meditation on Love

Mark Gabriele

For Bo & Becky

Love is invisible, but we know it is real by its effects. It creates. What it creates is more love, for where love is offered, love is returned. Because Love is both cause and effect, it magnifies itself–like ever-broader circles radiating in water from the smallest drop.

Love's eyes are different than ours. They do not discern or discriminate as ours do. Love sees with the heart and recognizes only its own creations as real. Love makes no judgments and therefore demands no justice; where there are boundaries it seeks to bridge them, where there are wrongs it seeks to forgive them, where there are hurts it seeks to heal them.

Love does not know time as we do–something that extinguishes itself passing from an uncertain future into an irreversible past. For Love, time–like everything else, has but one purpose– to increase love. Therefore Love knows only one time, the time when there is complete freedom for creation–the present moment. Fleeting for us, it is eternal for Love.

Love's math is different than ours. It understands how to add, and how to multiply–but not how to subtract, not how to divide. When it adds, it always makes one. What it adds, it multiplies.

Love knows nothing of degrees, nor how to measure. It only knows where it is, and where it is not. Where it is not, it longs to be created–and where it has been lost, it longs to be restored.

Love is simple, not sophisticated, and doesn't understand why it cannot be present in all places, at all times. Love doesn't understand what's impossible about bringing forth a child from an egg too small to see, why the deepest wound cannot heal, or why enemies cannot join together in peace. These things defy our sense of the world, so for us are miraculous. They are ordinary for Love.

Love fulfills who we are, and what we really want. It simply needs to be chosen. Whatever we mistakenly choose in its place is as certain to bring emptiness as choosing Love is to bring fulfillment. Yet all Love wants of a mistake is correction, and knows ulti- mately its purpose is assured.

All acts of love are equal in Love's eyes, so even the smallest one by our meas- urements is enough to open the doors to All of Heaven.

Copyright 2013 MIRAMBEL

Mirambel Publishing Company, LLC

ISBN 978-0-9856082-4-8
Library of Congress Control Number:
2012922377

Mirambel Publishing Company, LLC
PO Box 44
South Wellfleet, Massachusetts 02663
www.mirambelpublishing.com

Artwork photography by Dana Duke
Book and cover design by Kim Shkapich